YOU CHOOSE BOOKS

CAN YOU SURVIVE A

# GLOBAL BLACKOUT?

## An Interactive Doomsday Adventure

by MATT DOEDEN

illustrated by JAMES NATHAN

CAPSTONE PRESS
a capstone imprint

You Choose Books are published by Capstone Press,
1710 Roe Crest Drive, North Mankato, Minnesota 56003
www.capstonepub.com

**Library of Congress Cataloging-in-Publication Data**
Cataloging-in-publication information is on file with the Library of Congress.

ISBN 978-1-4914-5850-1 (library binding)
ISBN 978-1-4914-5923-2 (paperback)
ISBN 978-1-4914-5935-5 (eBook PDF)
978-1-4914-7874-5 (reflowable Epub)

**Editorial Credits**
Mandy Robbins, editor; Bobbie Nuytten, designer; Jo Miller, media researcher;
Kathey McColley, production specialist

**Photo Credits**
Shutterstock: javarman, (background,throughout), littleny, 109, photka, 106, Ronnie
Chua, 100, solarseven, 105

Printed in Canada.
032015    008825FRF15

# TABLE OF CONTENTS

# ABOUT YOUR
# ADVENTURE

YOU are living through a strange and dangerous time in Earth's near future. A civilization almost completely dependent on electricity is about to be brought to its knees. In the blink of an eye, the power upon which we rely is gone.

The lights wink out, and nobody knows why. In a moment, the world is thrust into darkness and chaos. How will you communicate and travel? Where will you get food and water? Can you survive and thrive after an unprecedented global blackout?

**YOU CHOOSE the path you take through a Global Blackout.**

# OUT GO THE LIGHTS

Your eyes are on the sky when it happens. It's sometime past 10 o'clock, and the light of your campfire flickers against the trees above. You're keeping an eye open for shooting stars. Next to you, your friend Tonya is in the middle of one of her famous ghost stories. A radio plays your favorite pop station in the background.

A chill runs down your spine just as the lights in the cabin flicker and blink out. The radio goes silent. Even the flashlight Tonya is holding up to her face as she tells the story blinks out.

Instantly, the sky seems to transform. Before, you'd been able to see a few dozen stars. Now, the night sky lights up with thousands … millions. The Milky Way stretches out before you, vivid in a way you've never before seen.

*Turn the page.*

"Whoa," says Tonya. "Power outage! This happens out here a lot. I think the power lines are old."

You stare up, ignoring Tonya as she resumes her story. You've never seen a sky like this. Not even close.

"I don't think it's the power lines."

"Huh?" says Peter, Tonya's twin brother. "What do you mean?"

"Look," you answer, pointing up. "Have you ever seen a sky like that?"

"Yeah, beautiful. But what does that have to do with the power outage?"

"Think about it, Peter. If it was just here, all the other towns and cities nearby would still be filling the sky with light. This must be a lot more widespread. And what about the radio and the flashlight? Those use batteries. I don't think they all just happened to die at the same moment the lights went out."

"Probably just a solar flare," Tonya says. "Those are supposed to be able to wipe out power."

"Nah," Peter blurts. "It's ALIENS! They're coming for us!"

The three of you laugh. But in truth, you've got a queasy feeling inside. This isn't right. And then you realize … there's not the sound of a single car or truck. There's a major highway less than a mile away. You should be able to hear cars.

"What time were your parents coming back?" you ask Tonya.

"Eleven," she says, looking at her watch. Don't worry, it's only 10:47."

You sigh. "Is the second hand on your watch moving?"

"Umm … ugg. No. Don't tell me this blackout thing ruined my watch! Now I'm mad!"

"My cell phone is dead too!" Peter says. You and Tonya check your phones, and they are both dead as well.

"What should we do?" Tonya asks.

***Turn the page.***

"What can we do?" Peter says.

"Let's just let the fire burn down and go to bed. Maybe everything will be working again in the morning," Tonya answers.

In time, the fire burns down. You put it out with a pail of water and head to bed.

In the morning, there's still no sign of Tonya and Peter's parents. And no power. Tonya stares blankly at her dead mobile phone.

"We need to find our parents," Peter says. "Dad will know what to do."

You're not so sure. There's food and water here. If there's been some major power failure, this is as good a spot to wait it out as you're likely to find. Tonya starts stuffing supplies into a backpack. "You coming?" she asks.

**To go with Tonya and Peter, go to page 11.**
**To wait out the blackout here, turn to page 14.**

You look back at the cabin. It seems like a safe place to wait things out. But if your friends are going, you're going too.

"They were going to a movie. The theater is in Mapleton." Tonya points west. "*That* way."

It's strange walking down the highway. It's mostly empty, but you pass a few stalled cars. A young man sits on the tailgate of a pickup truck. He waves as you approach. "Name's Trevor. Any idea what this is all about? Truck's dead. Phone's dead. And not a single car or truck has passed by."

"Seems to be some sort of massive blackout," you answer. "No power anywhere."

"Yeah, that's what I thought. Can't say I'm surprised."

"You're not?" Tonya asks.

"Not really. Just got out of the Army a few months ago. I saw things … weapons. Ever hear of an EMP?"

"What's an EMP?" Peter asks.

***Turn the page.***

"Electromagnetic pulse," says Trevor. "Basically, a huge bomb, but with no explosion. Knocks out everything electrical within its range. This must have been a big one. I'm betting it was terrorists."

You invite Trevor to join you, but he declines. "Think I'll hang out here for awhile. Hate to think of leaving my truck behind. But hey, if you're headed to Mapleton, I passed a bike shop a couple miles to the south. Might be worth checking out."

Tonya looks at you. "Let's do it. My feet are killing me!"

Peter shakes his head. "What's the point? It'll probably be closed, and we don't have much money anyway."

The twins look at you.

*To take a detour to the bike shop, turn to page 28.*
*To stay on foot, turn to page 30.*

"I'm staying put. My parents know I'm here. Home may be hundreds of miles away, but if they come looking, I want them to find me. We have food and water to last a week. Surely this will be over by then."

Tonya gives you a sour look. "Fine. Stay. We're going."

There's no talking her out of it. You're sorry to watch them leave, and you watch the road for a long time, half expecting them to come back.

The cabin is pretty remote. There are a few others on the lake, but no one is home. Your only company is Peter's dog Buster. The old golden retriever is 13 years old, half blind, and limps with arthritis. Peter hadn't wanted to leave him behind, but Tonya thought Buster would be better off here with you. Looking around the empty yard, you realize you're glad for the company.

"Don't know how long we might be here," you tell the dog. "What are we going to do with ourselves?"

*To get to work collecting supplies, turn to page 16.*
*To conserve your energy, turn to page 18.*

There's lots to do. The cabin's water is drawn from a well, but with no electricity, the pump won't run. Luckily they've also got an old-fashioned hand-pump in the back yard. You start to pump the rusty, creaky old thing. The water is rusty and dirty at first. But after awhile, it begins to clear. You fill several buckets. After giving one to Buster, you bring the rest inside.

Next it's time to gather firewood. The electrical heat is out, so it'll be the wood fireplace that keeps you warm at night. After a dozen back-breaking trips, you've got a nice stack of wood by the fireplace.

You're getting hungry. You head into the kitchen to take stock. After Tonya and Peter took what they could carry, there's little canned or dried food. The fridge has fruit, hamburger, bread, milk, and more. But already things are beginning to spoil. You eat some grapes and drink several tall glasses of milk, knowing that it will be the first thing to go bad.

You spend the rest of the day taking inventory. You've got a canoe, lots of fishing gear, and a first aid kit. You also find Tonya's father's stash of heavy-duty firecrackers. You chuckle, thinking how silly they seem now. All in all, you'll be set for a week or so. "Not bad," you tell Buster, looking over your survival gear.

That evening, you build a small fire and cook the remaining hamburger. Buster snores under your camp chair. Suddenly, the sound of shattering glass interrupts the quiet night. You stand up with a start. Your heart is racing. Faintly, you can hear voices. They're coming from the cabin next door. Someone is breaking in! What if they come this way next?

*To light a firecracker in hopes of scaring away the invaders, turn to page 19.*
*To hide, turn to page 21.*

There's no point in running yourself ragged right away. Best to conserve energy. You lay down in Peter's hammock and let the late-morning sun lull you to sleep. With a whine, Buster curls up beneath you.

It's late afternoon by the time you wake up. You stretch and head into the cabin's small kitchen. There, you open a can of baked beans and eat a cold supper. Buster whines at you until you remember to fill his bowl with dog food.

It's a beautiful night. You and Buster stroll out toward the main road to look at the stars. The night sky continues to amaze you. Maybe turning off the world's power isn't such a bad thing.

As you turn back to the cabin, you hear voices shouting and laughing. Buster begins to growl.

"Easy boy," you whisper. Who could this be out in the middle of the night?

*To head their direction to greet them, turn to page 24.*
*To get off the road where you can see who it is first,*
*turn to page 26.*

You scowl. Just 24 hours into the blackout and already people are stealing! The box of firecrackers is right inside the front door. Quickly, you dart inside, grab a lighter and one firecracker, and rush back out. The fuse hisses as you light it, then throw the firecracker a safe distance away.

CRRRRAAAAACK! The noise echoes through the still night air, sounding just like gunfire. For a moment, all is silent. Then you hear the voices again. But now they're moving away, and quickly.

"Off to find easier targets, I'm sure," you tell Buster. The dog stares up at you for a moment, then lays his head down and goes back to sleep.

*Turn the page.*

You sleep that night with a baseball bat at your side, but all is quiet. So too are the next several days. Five days after the power first blinked off, there's no end in sight. And you still haven't spoken to a soul since Tonya and Peter left. You're getting lonely, terribly worried, and your food stores are gone. You've managed to catch a few fish, but they're small and they don't go far. You've even started cutting back on Buster's food, knowing that, in a pinch, you could survive on that.

"I don't think anybody is coming for us," you tell Buster. He just looks up at you and whines. He's getting hungry too.

**To leave the cabin in search of people, turn to page 46.**
**To stick it out here, turn to page 49.**

You're alone out here. The last thing you want is a confrontation. You slip into the house, locking the door behind you. You sit there in darkness. Seconds pass. Minutes.

And then, footsteps. The doorknob on the front door rattles. Moments later, the sound of splintering wood as the door is kicked in. *They're coming inside!*

You back into the shadows. What can you do? As the door swings open, four figures rush inside.

"Not another step or I'll shoot," you say, your voice quivering.

The figures freeze. "Hey now, don't get crazy," says a voice. It sounds like a teenage boy.

"It's a bluff," says another. "There's no gun."

For a moment, all you can hear is their heavy breathing. At least one of them suspects that you're bluffing. But they can't be sure.

"Don't try me," you say, trying to keep your voice steady.

*Turn the page.*

With a growl, one of the figures turns. "Come on," he tells his partners in crime. But before he leaves, he turns toward you. "Don't think this is over. We know where you live now."

You barely sleep that night. Those words haunt you. The boy could have just been talking out of anger. But it felt *personal*. It's time to pack up and go. You can't stand the idea of constantly having to look over your shoulder.

*To attempt the long voyage home, turn to page 42.*
*To go in search of Tonya and Peter, turn to page 55.*

Better to tackle this head-on than hide from it.
With Buster on your heels, you step onto the road
and stride toward the group.

"Whoa, who's there?" shouts a voice.

"Ha, it's just a *kid*," says another with a cackle.

Four boys, probably around 17 or 18, quickly
surround you. "We don't know you," says one.
"What are you doing out here? It's not safe for kids,
you know."

"Just out for a stroll," you answer, trying to
remain calm.

"Let's get rid of the kid, Kyle. So we can … you
know … get on with business."

The apparent leader, Kyle, gives the other an angry
stare. "Shut your mouth."

Kyle gives you a long look. "So here's the thing, kid. We're going to knock off some of these tourist cabins tonight. Take anything worth anything. You got guts walking up to us in the middle of the night. I like that. Most kids would have done the smart thing and hid."

Kyle looks back over his shoulder. You can tell the other three boys are just waiting for him to decide what to do.

"So now you know my name and my plan. Here's a one-time only offer. You care to join us?"

*To join Kyle's group in robbing the local cabins,*
*turn to page 86.*
*To refuse, turn to page 90.*

"Shhhh Buster," you whisper, leading the dog off the road and into the trees. You crouch down behind some bushes and watch.

Four figures are approaching. You can see that at least two of them are carrying bats or hatchets. They appear to be teenagers, not much older than you.

"...Lots of good stuff this way," one voice says. "Cabins. People aren't around. Should be easy pickings."

They're planning to burglarize the cabins!

You watch the figures pass, then follow at a distance. Your heart sinks as they turn toward Tonya and Peter's cabin. But they enter a neighbor's cabin first. You hear the shattering of glass as they break in.

You've got to think fast. They're probably going to hit Tonya and Peter's place next. Do you dare risk running inside to grab what you can?

*To clear out and hope they don't take everything,*
*turn to page 40.*
*To rush into the cabin to gather supplies,*
*turn to page 80.*

A bike would be nice. "Let's do it," you say. Tonya grins while Peter rolls his eyes. Trevor points you toward a little county road and wishes you luck.

Half an hour later, you're staring at Jim's Bike Shop and Repair. The store looks like a big tin shed in the middle of the country. Bikes in various stages of repair line the outside of the shop.

"Hello!" you shout. No answer.

"Great," says Peter. "Like I said, nobody here."

"It's a big place Peter," Tonya barks. "Let's check around first."

Near the main entrance, a lineup of 10-speed bicycles catches your eye. "Check these out!" But as you look at the shiny bikes, your heart sinks. They're marked at $500 apiece! "Never mind. We can't afford these."

"No so fast," Peter says, pointing to the bike rack. "No locks on those."

"We can't *steal* them, Peter!" Tonya scolds.

"Of course not. We're not thieves. But we could *borrow* them. And bring them back when we're done with them, of course."

You know Tonya is right. It's stealing. But there's nobody here, and biking would be so much easier than walking.

*To side with Tonya, turn to page 32.*
*To side with Peter and take the bikes,*
*turn to page 84.*

You don't see much point in looking at bikes you can't afford. "Let's just keep moving."

The journey is long. But the three of you are young and in good shape. Before long, you're putting the miles behind you at a great pace.

Out in the country, it's almost possible to forget for a minute that there's no power, anywhere. The birds and bugs and fields of grain seem unbothered by the big blackout. The three of you chatter away happily, confident that all will return to normal soon.

"What's that?" Peter asks, pointing north. There's a thin trail of dark smoke on the horizon. A distant field looks scarred and torn apart. Glints of metal shine in the sunlight.

You squint your eyes. "I … I think that's an airplane. A crash. Oh no. I never even thought about what might happen to an airplane in the sky when everything went out."

*To investigate the crash, turn to page 34.*
*To continue on your way, turn to page 38.*

"The power's only been out a day. It's not time to steal and loot just yet. Let's look around a bit more."

Peter grumbles, but follows as you and Tonya lead the way. Around the back of the shop, you finally find Jim. "Hello," you call.

The man, middle-aged and wearing overalls, jumps. "Oh, you startled me." he says. "Sorry, but we haven't been able to do any business since the power went out. Can't even get the register to open."

"We could really use some help, sir," you explain. You tell Jim your story—three kids stranded and far from their parents. "Isn't there anything you could do?"

Jim scratches a scruffy beard. "Well, tell you what. I've got a few bikes out back here. Use them for spare parts and such. But they're all in working order. You want 'em, they're all yours."

With a heartfelt thank-you, the three of you are pedaling down the road. They're not luxury bikes by any means. But they get the job done. In just a few hours, you're pedaling into Mapleton.

The three of you stop on Main Street and look around. Some people have set up a small outdoor market that is buzzing with activity. Candles light several windows. It almost makes you think of a small frontier town from the 1800s.

The three of you ask around town. But nobody seems to have any idea where—or who—Peter and Tonya's parents are. If they were here, it seems that they're long gone.

"I'm sure they headed back for the cabin," Tonya says. "We should ride back. If we don't leave soon, we won't make it before dark."

You protest. The last thing you want is to go back out onto the road, and you feel safe here. But they're determined.

"We're going," Peter says. "Are you coming or not?"

*To stay in Mapleton, turn to page 44.*
*To return with Peter and Tonya, turn to page 70.*

The wreckage of the small crash is still burning. "Watch your step," Tonya scolds. Behind you, a strip of wheat field is torn and scorched where the small aircraft came down.

You and Peter are looking at broken sections of wing when you hear it. A cough? At first, you think it's your imagination. But then you hear it again. Someone's alive!

You rush toward the sound and pull away a fragment of the fuselage. There, lying in the wreckage, is a survivor! The woman, her face battered and bruised, looks at you and closes her eyes.

Minutes later, Tonya is holding a water bottle to the woman's lips. Her name is Rita, and she's an aviation student at a nearby university. "Leg's broken in a few places," she whispers, her voice hoarse. "Wouldn't have lasted long if you hadn't come. Thank you."

"What happened?" Peter asks.

*Turn the page.*

Rita tells you her story. "I was alone, practicing my instrument flying," she says. "It was really dark. In the distance, far beyond the horizon, I saw three distinct pulses of light. Pop … pop … pop. Then a second later, everything went down. I could literally see the entire countryside blink off in the wink of an eye. My instrument panel went black. I was 2,000 feet up in pitch blackness, and my engine was dead."

Your mouth hangs open at the thought. It's a miracle she didn't slam nose-first into the ground!

"I need to get back to the university, to tell them what I saw. Maybe that will make sense to someone who can help."

"We have to help her," you say to Peter and Tonya.

"Let's get her to Mapleton then. They've got a hospital there."

"No," Rita says. "Please, I need to get back to the university. Mapleton is in the opposite direction."

"We have to go to Mapleton to find our parents," Peter says. Tonya nods in agreement.

You have a decision to make.

**To bring Rita back to the university, turn to page 66.**
**To stick with Peter and Tonya, turn to page 38.**

"Come on," you say. "Let's keep moving."

Just before sunset, the three of you finally arrive. It's dark in town. No streetlights. No brightly lit windows. Just the flicker of candles here and there. A few people move about on the streets, but it's mostly quiet.

For about an hour, the three of you wander the streets, searching for signs of the twins' parents. But you see no sign of them or their car. "They're not here," you tell Peter with a frown.

You spend the night in the basement of a church, where cots are set up for those stranded by the blackout. No one has any idea what happened. Some say it was terrorism. Others think it was a solar flare or exploding star. At least one old woman at the shelter is convinced it's a punishment from God, while her husband insists it's a reward. Yet no real answers.

"There's nothing here for us," Tonya says the next day. "We need to start heading back."

*Turn to page 70.*

You're unarmed and alone. You don't want anything to do with these teenagers. You slink back into the woods, with Buster. About a football field's distance from the cabin, you stop. The sounds of shattering glass ring through the night.

You spend a cold, terrifying night huddled in the trees. At dawn, you muster the courage to leave your hiding spot. They did quite a number on the cabin. Windows are broken. The door hangs off of the hinges. Every drawer in the place has been torn out. And worst of all, just about everything useful or valuable is gone.

There's nothing here for you now.

With only the clothes on your back, you head for the road. You call to Buster several times. But the old dog refuses to leave. It's probably for the best. He'd only slow you down. You give him a final pat on the head. "Good luck old fella," you tell him.

*To head for the nearest town in search of answers, go to page 41.*
*To begin the long journey home, turn to page 42.*

Your home is more than 250 miles away. With no food or supplies, your chances of making it seem faint. So you resolve to head to the closest town, about 12 miles away. There's a university there. Maybe somebody knows what has happened.

As you walk, you pass countless abandoned cars and trucks. They sit on the road, useless. Why? It doesn't make any sense. You shake your head.

Several miles down the road, you spot a delivery truck in the ditch. The name of a local bakery is painted on the side. Your stomach growls at the thought of some donuts, rolls, or even just a loaf of bread. You try the doors, but they're locked. So is the back of the truck. You groan.

*To continue on your journey, turn to page 62.*
*To try to break into the delivery truck,*
*turn to page 69.*

You know the road will be long and difficult, but there's only one place you want to go. Home.

As the sun rises on a cool morning, you begin the voyage. The landscape feels almost alien. Trucks and cars sit abandoned on the highways. A deer stands grazing on the side of the road. Fires burn in the distance.

Shortly after noon, you notice a small group ahead. About a dozen people, old and young, are traveling together. They wave to you.

"Where you heading?" asks a woman carrying an infant. She introduces herself as Sarah.

"South. Home," you answer.

"Well we're heading south for a stretch as well. It's safer traveling in numbers. As the days without power stretch on, people are getting desperate. Travel with us."

You look the group over. Men. Women. Several children. They'll slow you down, but company is nice.

*To travel with the group, turn to page 74.*
*To strike out on your own, turn to page 78.*

"Look, I get that you want to find your parents. And we tried. But Mapleton looks a lot safer than the open road right now. I want to stay and see what I can learn about what's going on. Maybe someone here can help us get home eventually."

You can't talk them out of leaving though. So you wish them well as they turn around and hit the road again. "Come back if you can," you tell them.

Mapleton isn't a bustling city. It's small, quiet, and laid back. You stroll to the little street market. "Can I help you?" asks an elderly woman sitting behind a table of tomatoes, radishes, and other produce.

"Looking for a place to stay. My home is a long way away and I don't have much to my name, but I'm willing to work."

"Well, a strong youngster like yourself is always welcome on my farm. It's just a half mile out of town. Room and board, and in exchange you help with housework and chores."

"Just until all of this blows over, right?" you ask.

"Oh dear, I'm afraid this isn't going to blow over. This is sent from above. A higher power. My preacher says so. He'll tell you himself tonight at the farm over supper. What do you say?"

*To accept, turn to page 95.*
*To decline the invitation, turn to page 98.*

"This isn't going away, is it boy?" you ask Buster. You had hoped to wait things out in safety here, but it's quickly becoming clear that you could be waiting a very, very long time.

With the decision made, you act quickly. You pack up everything you can find that might be useful. You sling two backpacks worth of supplies and gear over your shoulder and get to bed early. At dawn, you're off, heading down the road in search of people.

It's slow going. Buster tags alongside you, but he's old and slow. You take frequent rests to keep him fresh.

You're amazed how a week without power changes things. No cars or trucks rumbling down the road. No blinking billboards. No traffic lights. And what few fellow travelers you do see tend to keep their distance. Everything just feels *strange*.

Several miles down the road, you come to a gas station. The place looks abandoned. The doors hang open, but there's no sign of movement inside. "Let's check it out," you tell Buster.

*Turn the page.*

The smell hits you as soon as you enter. Rot and decay. With no power, all the refrigerated food has spoiled. You pull your shirt up over your nose and poke around. There's no unspoiled food or water left. The place has been ransacked. As you turn to leave, you notice a display with maps. You grab one. You don't know the area well, and it could come in handy.

Outside, in fresh air, you inspect the map carefully. The area is pretty isolated. There's a small town about 4 miles east. There's a bigger one about 15 miles west. You're pretty sure that's the direction Tonya and Peter went in search of their parents.

**To head for the small town nearby, turn to page 51.**
**To go west in search of your friends, turn to page 55.**

The only people you've heard in the past five days were breaking into a nearby cabin. No, you don't trust strangers right now. Better to stay here, all alone.

You spend your days fishing and trapping small game. Squirrel doesn't taste very good. But it's better than Buster's dog food, which is quickly dwindling. Days turn into weeks, which turn into months. The warmth of summer begins to fade. The first snow falls on the same day that Buster passes away. Maybe in the spring you'll try to make your way back home. With your newly developed survival skills the 250-mile journey doesn't seem as impossible as it once did.

On several occasions, you hear people nearby. Fearful, you stay out of sight. To your relief, no one approaches the cabin.

*Turn the page.*

As winter grows colder and colder, life becomes more difficult. The lake freezes over. The squirrels, rabbits, and other small game you've been trapping become more scarce. You're almost always hungry and cold. You don't have the energy needed to cut and haul enough firewood.

On a late January morning, you're inside, huddled in blankets, when you again hear voices outside. "Anyone here? Anyone?"

**To call out, turn to page 58.**
**To remain hidden behind locked doors, turn to page 60.**

FRANKLIN

POPULATION: 59

"Fifty-nine," you mutter to yourself as you trudge into the tiny town. "Sheesh."

There isn't much to Franklin. A handful of homes, many of which look abandoned. Railroad tracks lead into town, heading past its biggest feature, a grain elevator. You're staring up at it when a shot rings out.

You freeze in place as a man's voice up ahead shouts out. "Stop where you are. Don't want to hurt you, but we can't tolerate strangers these days."

"Don't shoot!" you shout back. "I'm just looking for information."

You take a tentative step forward when another shot rings out. "I mean it. Not a step closer!"

*Turn the page.*

Then another voice—a woman's. "Stop it right now Edward Thompson!" A woman of perhaps 60 years strides across the town's main street, headed your direction. "Can't you see this is a child? What kind of people would we be turning away a child?"

The woman wraps her arm around your shoulder and leads you to a small white house. "Come along now. Let's get you something to eat. I'm sorry it wasn't a warmer welcome. You'll have to excuse Ed. We've had some … trouble with strangers. This blackout has people behaving very poorly."

It's a whirlwind of an afternoon. You soon discover that the 59 printed on the town's sign is a generous count. Within a day, you meet most of the people still calling Franklin home, including Ed Thompson, who sheepishly apologizes for his rude introduction. But of all the people, your favorite by far is Rose, the woman who came to your rescue. She's a widow whose kids are several states away in college.

*Turn the page.*

"Stay with us," Rose tells you. "You're young and strong. We need people like you. We've plenty of food. And the people here are good—even Ed. Stay here, until all of this blackout nonsense is over."

It's an easy decision. You agree to stay for now. You can help here. You can feel safe here. In these times, that's all anyone can ask. Rose and the others seem to believe it's only a matter of time before things return to normal. But at night, staring up at the starry sky, you're not so sure. Will you ever make it home to see your parents again?

## THE END

*To follow another path, turn to page 10.*
*To learn more about global blackouts, turn to page 101.*

"Let's go find your family," you tell Buster. The old dog wags his tail happily. You can almost believe he understands you.

You strike off to the west, hoping that you're following in Tonya's and Peter's footsteps. They were headed toward the city of Mapleton, where their parents had been when everything went dark.

Several miles down the road, you're overcome with the sense that you're being watched. You stop, looking all around you. But you can't see anything but farmland. Rows and rows of corn, wheat, and other crops. You shake your head and continue. That's when you hear it—rustling leaves. Somebody is in the field, pacing you.

"Show yourself!" you shout. "I know you're there."

Two figures emerge. The faces and clothing are dirty. The hair is matted. Each stands about half your height. They're children!

*Turn the page.*

"Hello there," you say, kneeling down. The kids come closer. It's a boy and a girl, about 5 years old. "Where are your parents?"

The girl shrugs. "Dad's gone. Mom left for food. She never came back."

"You're here all alone?"

They both nod. The girl points across a cornfield. A small farmhouse stands on a hill. "That's our house."

The children, Anna and Jeremy, are twins. They lead you back to their house. The place is a mess. Toys and empty food containers lie everywhere. "The food is almost gone," Anna says. The kids have been surviving on cereal, granola bars, and apples from a tree outside.

You ask them if they want to come with you, but they both refuse to leave the house. "Mom might come back," Jeremy explains. Somehow, you doubt it.

*To wish them well and continue on your journey,*
*turn to page 91.*
*To stay here and help them, turn to page 93.*

You're still wary of people, but you have no choice. You're not going to survive the winter alone. You pull yourself to your feet and shuffle to the cabin's front door. You slide the latch, then crack the door open.

"In here," you call out, coughing.

Two figures stand outside, dressed in heavy coats, hats, and scarves. It takes a moment before you recognize them. "Dad! Mom!" You stumble out into the cold winter air, falling into you father's arms.

All three of you are in tears as you bring them inside and tell them your story. In turn, they tell theirs. Your town, like many others, came together after the blackout. With communications down, federal and state governments crumbled. Cities and towns had to fend for themselves. Your parents played a big part in organizing your hometown.

"I'm sorry it took us so long to find you," your mother says. "At first, we thought it was a passing thing. Then it was just a struggle to survive. It took months of planning just to get here, and we didn't know if you'd even be here when we arrived. But we had to try."

You give her a big hug, more thankful than you've ever been in your life.

"What is it? What caused it?" you ask, finally.

"Nobody knows," your father answers. "And if they do, there's no way for them to tell the world. Everything is down. Phones, the Internet, everything. It's like some cosmic force just sent us back to the dark ages. Whether it's an act of God or nature, it seems permanent. It's a new world. Let's get a good night's sleep here tonight. Tomorrow we start the long journey back home."

## THE END
*To follow another path, turn to page 10.*
*To learn more about global blackouts, turn to page 101.*

You freeze. You're almost afraid to even breathe. In your months of isolation, you've grown more and more paranoid and fearful.

More footsteps. The doorknob turns and rattles. A voice calls out again, "Hello?" For a moment you think you recognize the voice, but that's probably your stressed mind playing tricks on you. Finally, you hear the footsteps moving away. Whoever that was must have given up.

You shiver, though you're not sure if it's from fear of that close call or the chill in the cabin. Your fire is barely embers. You groan and stand up, reaching for another log. But your pile is empty. You'll have to go out for more.

Not now though. You're so tired, so cold. And who knows if there are still people around? No, you just lay back down and close your eyes.

It's a bitterly cold night. The temperature inside the cabin plummets. You fall asleep shivering violently. You do not wake up.

## THE END

*To follow another path, turn to page 10.*
*To learn more about global blackouts, turn to page 101.*

.No distractions. You leave the truck behind and continue on your way. Your stomach growls, but you know that a person can go days without food.

It's mid afternoon when you finally reach town. At the university, a crowd is gathered on the main lawn. All eyes are on a woman who appears to be giving a demonstration. She's wrapping bandages on a young man whom you imagine is a college student.

"What's going on?" you ask an elderly man standing in the back.

"Nursing professor," he whispers. "This is the first aid seminar."

The two of you speak quietly. It turns out that the university staff is doing what it can to help people get through this crisis. The nursing department is showing people how to treat simple injuries and illnesses. The engineering department is teaching citizens how to build things such as water wheels and windmills. The school's wrestling coach is even giving a seminar in self defense.

"Do they know what's going on? Why this is happening?"

The man gives you a long look. "Let's walk," he says.

The man, you learn, is Dr. Watkins, the chair of the university's physics department. He talks as he leads you to his office, a small, cramped room lined with bookshelves. "There are a hundred theories," he tells you. "Most people here are convinced it was some sort of massive solar flare or supernova. But I don't buy it. Neither event explains it."

He pulls a slender volume from the top drawer of his desk and opens it to an earmarked page. "This is a journal of physics. It describes an experiment at a European supercollider. Basically, a team of physicists was trying to discover the universe's most elementary particle. The building block of everything—energy, matter, gravity—the whole she-bang."

*Turn the page.*

You listen to his theory. Dr. Watkins thinks the physicists did something, opened up some previously locked door to one of the universe's deep dimensions—dimensions so small that human beings didn't even know that they existed. And in doing so, they accidentally hacked the universe, changing one or more of its most basic laws.

The two of you strike up an unlikely friendship. You talk about physics, life, and the universe. "I don't have any family of my own now," Dr. Watkins tells you. "And it seems that neither do you. Not many people interested in higher physics right now. I could sure use a student … and apprentice. Care to make the university your home for now?"

It doesn't take you more than a heartbeat to agree. If you can't be home, you can't think of any place else you'd rather be. You grin, stick out your hand, and tell Dr. Watkins, "It's a deal."

## THE END
*To follow another path, turn to page 10.*
*To learn more about global blackouts, turn to page 101.*

"What Rita saw, what she's been through. I can't just leave her," you tell your friends. They're disappointed, but they understand. "We'll find you when this is all over," Tonya promises, giving you a hug. You hope they find their parents.

Rita's wounds aren't life-threatening—at least not yet. But her leg is broken and she can't put weight on it. You find some sturdy sticks to build a splint for her leg and make a crude crutch. She hobbles along, but it's slow-going and painful. About a mile down the road, you spot an abandoned pickup truck loaded with landscaping supplies, including a wheelbarrow.

You get Rita into the wheelbarrow and comfortable. Soon, you're back on the road, making much better time. The two of you travel north for three more days. You survive wind, rain, and hunger. You marvel at the stars. By the time you arrive at the university, Rita feels like a dear old friend.

*Turn the page.*

The university is buzzing with activity. Professors put on free seminars for the public. An engineer shows people how to build windmills and water wheels. Nurses provide first aid training. Scientists gather to discuss possible causes of the crisis. Rita's account of three flashes of light before the blackout sparks intense debate. Some argue that it must have been a nuclear strike. Others say it was an EMP. A third group says neither explanation makes any sense.

You love the vibrant life here. But you need a roof over your head and food to eat. Rita gets you a job with the school's agriculture department, helping to clean and maintain the department's greenhouse.

As the weeks stretch into months, you realize that the lights may not ever be coming back on. But life here goes on. You'll work and learn. And you'll keep your eyes on the horizon, waiting for the day you're reunited with friends and family.

## THE END

*To follow another path, turn to page 10.*
*To learn more about global blackouts, turn to page 101.*

If there's food in this truck, you need to get it. It hasn't even been a day since your last meal, and already you're feeling weak. You grab a large rock off the side of the road and heave it with all your might.

CRASH! The glass on the passenger-side window shatters into a thousand pieces. You reach inside to unlock the door when you hear the tiny clicking sound.

BOOM! The sound of gunfire startles you. It takes a moment to realize that the shot came from inside the truck! It takes a few moments more to realize that your abdomen is covered in blood.

"Out of my truck thief!" calls a man's voice.

You grunt in reply and slump to the ground. Inside, the man continues to shout. Soon, the sound of the man's crazed voice fades into the background. It disappears as you finally slip off into a sleep from which you'll never wake.

## THE END

*To follow another path, turn to page 10.*
*To learn more about global blackouts, turn to page 101.*

You hate to leave the safety and comfort of Mapleton behind you. But your friends won't rest until they've found their parents. So it's back on the road.

"There's a small county road that skirts the river. It's a longer way back to our cabin, but our folks might have taken the scenic route home. Let's head that way."

One thing is for sure, it's a much prettier road. And there's hardly any abandoned vehicles here. So when you do catch the glint of the sun on a windshield several miles out of town, hopes are raised.

"It's their car!" Tonya shouts, rushing toward it. You and Peter are right behind her.

The car is in rough shape. The front has slammed into a tree. No one is inside.

"Look," says Peter. "They must have been coming around that curve when the power went out. Poof! No lights. No power steering. Dad probably couldn't get it stopped in time, and they hit this tree. They have to be somewhere near."

*Turn the page.*

An hour later, you find them. They're huddled in an empty barn. Peter's dad, Tim, is unconscious. His mother, Beth, is scraped and bruised, but otherwise well. She breaks into tears at the sight of her children.

"Tim isn't well," she tells you later. "We walked here for shelter after the accident. But then he fell asleep, and I haven't be able to wake him. I couldn't bear to leave him, but he needs help. Can you call? My phone is out."

It's heartbreaking. She doesn't know. And now you're the one who has to tell her, no help is coming. At least not any time soon.

You begin to make plans to move Tim, to take him back to Mapleton. Peter starts work on a makeshift stretcher. But it's all too late. Tim passes away that night. You bury him in a shallow grave the following day.

You help the grieving family back to Mapleton later that day. The pastor of a local church agrees to take them in. Peter finds work with a local farmer. Tonya and her mother earn their keep helping around the church and the pastor's home.

The pastor asks if you would like to stay with them as well. But your mind is made up. You are determined to make your way home to your parents. Tonya, Peter, and their mother load you up with supplies and send you on your way. You hope you can make it home safely. And you hope to see your friends again some day too.

## THE END

*To follow another path, turn to page 10.*
*To learn more about global blackouts, turn to page 101.*

You give Sarah a smile and a nod. Traveling with people would be nice. After your ordeal at the cabin, having some friends around seems like a good idea.

It's slow going. But then, you're not on a deadline. The group shares their food with you, and one of the men, Horace, helps teach you how to hunt. On the first day, he shoots two rabbits and a squirrel. Sarah helps you identify edible plants in the ditches. You have dandelion and rabbit stew that night. You are quick to catch on and begin to enjoy honing your survival skills.

The world has changed quickly. Homes and entire towns lay in smoldering ruins. Part of you thinks you should try to help, but anything that slows you down could mean the difference between life and death. The people you meet are careful around you, distrustful of strangers. But no one bothers such a large group. And so you continue to move, mile after mile.

Three weeks later, you say tearful farewells. The members of the group are continuing south. But your home is just 20 miles east. Close now. Alone, you can probably make it in a day.

Yet you're filled with dread. Ahead, smoke billows in the sky. After all you've seen, you don't know what to expect when you reach home. Will your home even be there still? What about your family and friends? You'll find out soon. Ten miles to go. Now five. Now one. You can see some familiar rooftops rising in the distance.

As you enter your hometown, two armed men stand before you. "State your business," one barks. "We don't want any strangers here." You're startled and afraid, but you know that voice.

"Mr. Edwards?" you ask.

*Turn the page.*

It is Mr. Edwards, your English teacher! He doesn't recognize you at first. You realize that three weeks on the road has left you covered in grime. But as soon as he realizes it's you, he wraps you up in a big bear hug. "Your folks have been worried. Let's get you home! I'll bet you've got quite a story to tell."

You know life here is going to be nothing like what it was before the blackout. But you're home, surrounded by people you trust. You give Mr. Edwards a smile. "You have no idea."

## THE END

*To follow another path, turn to page 10.*
*To learn more about global blackouts, turn to page 101.*

Traveling with this many people will only slow you down. "Thanks for the invitation," you tell Sarah. "But I've got more than 200 miles to cover. I figure that alone, I can make 20 miles a day. That'll have me home in a couple weeks."

You wish Sarah and the others well, and then you're off. Alone again. Six days later, you figure you're almost halfway home. But as you cross a creek that afternoon, everything changes. It's a small stream, less than 5 feet across. You try to leap over it. But your foot lands awkwardly on a slick rock. You hear a sick crunching sound and feel a bolt of pain as you crash into the frigid water.

The pain almost overwhelms you. You lose consciousness for a moment, but the cold water soon brings you back. You drag yourself from the water into a heap on the shore. Your pants are soaked in cold water and warm blood.

You wince as you roll up the leg and see the damage.  A fragment of your leg bone juts out through the skin. Blood spurts out of the wound.

Desperately, you try to tie it off. You strip off your sweatshirt and try to wrap one of the sleeves tightly above the wound. But your fingers shake from cold and from shock, and you're already feeling light-headed. It takes you several tries just to make a knot, and when you finally do, you're too weak and out of it to pull it tight enough to cut of the blood flow.

Your makeshift tourniquet is a failure. And that means you're not going to make it home.

## THE END
*To follow another path, turn to page 10.*
*To learn more about global blackouts, turn to page 101.*

You need the food and supplies inside the cabin. Without them, you're in big trouble! "Stay here Buster," you say, then dart inside. In the dark, you grab for your backpack and start stuffing cans of food inside. You grab a sharp knife out of the drawer, a can of bug spray, binoculars, and a few other odd items that you stumble across.

It's not much, but at least you'll have something left. You rush toward the back door to slip out when a voice calls out, "Who's there?"

You wince. Too slow!

"Who's there. Talk now or this goes badly for you."

"I'm nobody," you answer. "Just take what you want. I don't care. I just want to be left alone."

Your voices draw in the others. One holds an old-fashioned lantern. In the dark, the flame is almost blinding. But you finally get a good look. Four teenage boys, and they don't look happy to see you.

"What are we gonna do Kyle?" asks one of the boys. Kyle, the kid who shouted the warning, gives him a glare. "Well, now we're using our names. Great idea Jim. Now we haven't got much choice."

You prepare to dart for the door. But as if reading your mind, Kyle moves between you and the door.

"Kyle, let it go," says another boy. "It's not worth it."

But Kyle takes a threatening step forward. Then another. You realize he's going to attack you! But before he does, the kid holding the lantern grabs him by the shoulder. "Kyle, enough!"

Kyle spins around, accidentally slamming into the other boy. The lantern flies from the boy's grasp. WHOOOSH! As the lantern smashes into the cabin's wood floor, flame leaps up. For a moment, all you can do is stare. As the lantern's oil spreads across the floor, the flame follows its path. In seconds, the cabin is filling with smoke. The curtains catch fire and the flames crawl up the walls.

*Turn the page.*

"Let's get out of here!" shouts a boy. Kyle is already half way out the door. The one he called Jim stares back at you. "I'm sorry," he says, then follows the others.

You're trapped. A wall of flame stands between you and the door. You spin and try to open a window. But it's jammed. You try to drive your elbow through the glass, but it won't budge. You pull your t-shirt up over your mouth, but it doesn't help. You're choking on the smoke. With one last lunge, you throw yourself into the window.

Nothing. You fall to the floor, doubled over, coughing. You reach a hand for the door, but it's hopeless. You just hope Buster will be okay.

## THE END

*To follow another path, turn to page 10.*
*To learn more about global blackouts, turn to page 101.*

"Look Tonya, Peter's right. We'll just bring the bikes back when we're done. No big deal."

You climb onto a bright green model, gripping the foam-lined handlebars and digging your feet into the pedals. You guide the bike out onto the paved drive. The ride is silky smooth. "Oh these are perfect!"

Tonya and Peter each pick a bike. "Okay, let's get out of here," Peter says.

But as you begin to pedal back toward the road, a voice rings out. "STOP! Thieves! Stop or I'll shoot!"

A quick glance over your shoulder reveals a middle-aged man, face marked with grease. He is running in your direction with a shotgun in his hands. He repeats his warning "Stop or I'll shoot!"

"He's bluffing," Peter says. "Go!"

You dig your feet into the pedals and spin them as fast as you can. A second passes. Two. Maybe Peter was right. Maybe the man … you assume it's Jim … is just bluffing.

You feel the shot before you hear it. It catches you square in the back. You fly off the bike head over heels, slamming into the ground violently. You hear a second shot before you pass out. You don't even have time to hope that there isn't a third one.

## THE END

*To follow another path, turn to page 10.*
*To learn more about global blackouts, turn to page 101.*

Four faces stare at you through the darkness. You're pretty sure that you know what your answer needs to be. "Let's go then," you say.

Kyle claps you on the back and breaks into a run. The first cabin the group hits is one of your friends' neighbors. They hurl a rock through a window to smash it, then reach inside to unlock the door. "You first," Kyle says with a sneer.

And so it goes. You go from house to house with the group, smashing windows and grabbing whatever you want to grab. Your plan is to slip away as soon as you get a chance. But then they hit Tonya and Peter's cabin. You pretend that you don't know the place, but watching the group ransack their stuff breaks your heart.

After you're done, Kyle leads the group back to an old abandoned barn. "This is where we're staying. With the power out, we cleared out of town, and we're not going back."

*Turn the page.*

You don't care much for your new companions, and you don't know where Buster ended up after that first night. But they've got food and shelter. The group—Kyle and half a dozen others—seems to accept you as one of their own.

*I'll stick with them just a few more days*, you tell yourself, hoping everything returns to normal soon. But that doesn't happen. Weeks pass. Things only seem to get worse. People are getting desperate, clashing violently for resources. Kyle's group grows bolder, raiding homes while people are still there.

A year after the blackout, you're with Kyle and some of the others, raiding a home on the outskirts of Mapleton. You're running, carrying your loot, when you slam headfirst into someone. You both go sprawling to the ground.

You're taken aback as you stand and realize that it's Peter! "Hey!" you shout, moving forward to grab your friend in a hug. But Peter shrinks back, then bolts away.

*He didn't even recognize me!* you think. *All he saw was a criminal.*

You think back to the last time you saw him, to the person you were before the world changed. And you realize that you barely recognize yourself anymore. And it's at that moment you decide. You stand up, brush yourself off, and walk straight out of town, away from the people you've been robbing, and away from Kyle and his gang. It's time to find a new way of life in this new world.

## THE END

*To follow another path, turn to page 10.*
*To learn more about global blackouts, turn to page 101.*

"My friends own one of these cabins you're talking about robbing," you say defiantly. "Take your crew of thieves and go somewhere else."

You're banking on Kyle respecting your bravery once again. No such luck. The boy hauls back and levels you with a punch to the face. Your head is spinning and your ears are ringing, but you're still conscious. At least long enough to see Kyle kneel over you and draw back his fist once again.

"Wrong answer," he says with a scowl.

## THE END
*To follow another path, turn to page 10.*
*To learn more about global blackouts, turn to page 101.*

"Look, kids. It's not safe for you to stay here alone. Find a neighbor. Tell them your parents are gone. I'm sure somebody will help you."

With that, you're on your way. As the day stretches on, you find your thoughts drifting back to that little farmhouse. Will the kids be okay? Should you have stayed?

Distracted, you fail to notice the large pothole in the middle of the road. Your ankle turns over with a sickening CRUNCH as you step into it. "Ahhhhhh!" you shout, falling to the pavement in agony.

It's bad. The bone is broken, you're sure. You can't put any weight on it at all. And now here you are, out in the middle of nowhere, unable to move. You pull yourself to the side of the road. That's where you spend a cold and miserable night. By morning, you're shivering from cold and the pain in your ankle.

Late the following morning, you spot movement. It's a horse! A lone rider approaches. A man, probably in his 30s or 40s. "Help!" you shout.

*Turn the page.*

The man approaches, then reigns the horse to a stop. Carefully, he steps down. "Looks like you're in a bad spot," he says.

"My ankle. I think I broke it. I need help."

The man stares down at you. Then his gaze turns to your backpack.

"Last person I helped tried to rob me," says the man. "I won't make that mistake again."

He snatches your backpack from your grasp. "I will make good use of this though. Good day to you."

You can't even muster up a tear as you watch him ride away with the last of your meager possessions. How can you expect someone to help you when you refused to help children who desperately needed it?

You lie back onto the ground. Maybe someone else will be along to help you. But you doubt it. At least you still have Buster staying by your side.

## THE END

*To follow another path, turn to page 10.*
*To learn more about global blackouts, turn to page 101.*

These kids need help. You're not about to leave them here alone.

"Let's work on getting this place cleaned up," you say. You give each child a job, and get to work taking stock. You soon realize that this is a perfect place to wait out a blackout. The fields are brimming with corn and wheat. Wild game such as pheasants and rabbits will be plentiful. And there's even fresh eggs from a small chicken coop. There's a wood-burning stove in the house to keep you warm when winter comes.

It takes a while for the kids to really trust you. But they're hard workers, and soon the three of you have a routine. In time, you meet several neighbors. People out here are pretty spread out, but you begin to build a real sense of community. Neighbors help each other. You learn to harvest the old-fashioned way, and to plant the following spring.

*Turn the page.*

A year after the blackout, you find yourself gazing to the south. Your parents are that way, somewhere. Perhaps someday you'll strike out again, in search of your family. But for now, this is your home. This is your family. And you think your parents would be proud of what you've done. Will the power ever come back on? You don't know. Either way, the world is changed forever. And as you gaze over the land, listening to the distant sounds of children at play, you're not really sure it's for the worse.

## THE END

*To follow another path, turn to page 10.*
*To learn more about global blackouts, turn to page 101.*

The farm is beautiful. Rolling fields, a little white house, a creaky old windmill in the back. The woman—Ms. Alexander—shows you to a room upstairs. "You'll sleep here, dear. Get yourself cleaned up and come down for supper in an hour."

You're surprised to find a dozen people downstairs. All are listening to one man—Reverend Elmer. The Reverend is a young man and a powerful speaker. He has everyone in the house convinced that this blackout is an act of God designed to punish sinners. And, he tells them, that God has personally chosen him to lead humanity back to its old ways. As he speaks, you can feel his gaze burning through you.

*This is a cult!* you realize. *Elmer has these people convinced he's their savior!*

*Turn the page.*

Soon, Elmer begins to tell the group about a way to cleanse themselves. You start to notice awkward glances from all around the room. One woman looks at you with … pity. You excuse yourself for the bathroom, then slip out the back door. You leave what few possessions you had behind and put as much distance between yourself and that cult as you can.

And so begins your life alone, on the road, post blackout. You know home is south, but you're not exactly sure how to get there. And you need to feed yourself in the meantime. You bounce from town to town, doing odd jobs, just scraping by. You hope you're on the right track and will find your home and your parents before the situation becomes desperate.

## THE END
*To follow another path, turn to page 10.*
*To learn more about global blackouts, turn to page 101.*

"Umm … thanks for the offer. Let me think about it." You hurry away from the stand, suddenly wary of the old woman.

Later that day, you meet the owner of a local grocery store. He offers to put you up in a spare room in exchange for work stocking shelves. You gladly accept, thinking it will be just a day or two. The work isn't hard, and the room is comfortable. But a few days soon becomes a few weeks, and still no power.

The townspeople grow more and more worried. You desperately want to go home, but you hear terrible tales from the road. Roving gangs violently taking all the resources they can. A strange cult out of town accused of capturing and enslaving travelers. A nearby town is burned to the ground.

Things just seem to get worse and worse. You join the town's makeshift militia to protect the town. Two nights a week, you patrol the town's borders, keeping strangers out.

A month passes. Lacking stock, the grocery store closes. You get by doing odd jobs and helping on local farms. The days are long and hard. You miss your friends and family, and you wonder what happened to Tonya and Peter.

Two months. A year. The days stretch on in this new life, without power. You do your best to survive, and you save up food and supplies. As soon as you think you have enough saved up you will set out to find your parents and get back home.

## THE END

*To follow another path, turn to page 10.*
*To learn more about global blackouts, turn to page 101.*

# AN ELECTRIC WORLD

Electricity. We live in a society that can't exist without it. We use it for almost everything we do. It drives everything from communication to transportation. Without it, we can't use a phone, turn on a computer, or even access our bank records. Farmers wouldn't be able to bring in the harvests that feed the world—at least not on the scale they do today. Modern medical devices would become useless. Turn off the power and the world as we know it ceases to exist.

Of course, that's not true everywhere. People in many poor nations would barely notice a difference. They don't rely on "the grid" the way Western society does. Turn off the power and life there would just keep going on as it has for centuries.

The events in this book are fiction. We don't really know of anything that could knock out all forms of power permanently. The characters in the book come up with all kinds of ideas on how it could happen, from science experiments gone wrong to an alien attack. But in truth, the type of permanent global blackout in this story doesn't seem very likely.

But what sort of event really could cause a widespread blackout? We can look to our nearest star, the sun, for an answer. A solar storm, or coronal mass ejection (CME), happens when the sun ejects huge volumes of its gas out into the solar system. If a big, powerful CME were to slam into Earth, it could bring down the entire power grid. The damage could linger for days, weeks, months, or maybe even years.

And CMEs are not the stuff of science fiction. In 1859 a huge CME brought down telegraph systems all over North America and Europe. In 1989 the city of Quebec, Canada, was thrown into darkness by a CME. Millions of people were without power for nine hours. And in 2012 a CME narrowly missed hitting Earth. In 2014 Professor Daniel Baker, director of the University of Colorado's Laboratory for Atmospheric and Space Physics said, "If it had hit, we would still be picking up the pieces," .

Closer to home, the electromagnetic pulse (EMP) is a top candidate for causing a major blackout. An EMP is an ultra-powerful burst of radiation. The radiation can damage or even destroy electronics.

Lightning is one type of small EMP. Think about it. If lightning strikes a building … BLINK! Off goes the power. TVs, computers, and other electronics can be fried. Now think bigger.

It's possible to build a device that emits a powerful EMP. If a hostile nation or terrorist group were to take the idea to the extreme, it's not impossible to imagine a pulse, or series of pulses, that could send a nation or region right back into the Stone Age.

Could events like these really happen? You bet. In fact, scientists say that a CME event is certain to happen at some time. It's just a matter of when, where, and how strong. Will such an event wipe out the entire global power grid? Probably not. But it doesn't hurt to be ready.

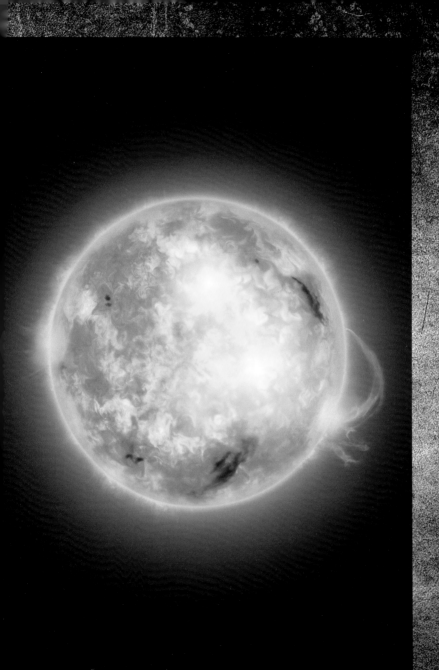

# GLOBAL BLACKOUT SURVIVAL GUIDE

   Suppose a massive CME is on a collision course with Earth. What do you do? How would you survive in a world where the lights—and everything else that needs power—suddenly flickered and blinked off? What sort of items might help you make it through such a shocking and turbulent transition? Here's a survival pack!

*FIRST AID KIT WITH STERILE BANDAGES

*QUALITY HAND TOOLS SUCH AS HAMMERS, WRENCHES, AND SCREWDRIVERS. POWER TOOLS ARE WORTHLESS WITHOUT POWER!

*WILDERNESS SURVIVAL BOOK. YOU'RE GOING TO NEED TO LEARN TO START FIRES, IDENTIFY EDIBLE AND MEDICINAL PLANTS, TRAP ANIMALS, AND BUTCHER WHAT YOU CATCH. A SURVIVAL BOOK CAN TEACH YOU HOW TO DO ALL OF THESE THINGS.

*PAPER AND WRITING UTENSILS. YOUR PHONE WON'T WORK ANYMORE, SO YOU'LL HAVE TO GO OLD SCHOOL IF YOU WANT TO SEND A MESSAGE.

*CANNED OR DEHYDRATED FOOD

*BOTTLED WATER

*FLINT OR LIGHTER TO START FIRES

*HUNTING AND/OR FISHING GEAR

*MAP. NO MORE GPS. NO MORE GOOGLE!

*FLASHLIGHT AND BATTERIES

*CANDLES. LOTS OF CANDLES.

# TEN TIPS TO SURVIVE
# A GLOBAL BLACKOUT

- Stay calm. Panic causes people to make bad choices and take unnecessary risks.

- Determine what supplies you need, collect them, and prepare to wait it out. You will want to include at least two weeks worth of food and water.

- Learn basic first aid information—have a first aid kit, and know how to use it.

- Learn how to hunt and trap animals and/or grow your own food. Once your food supply runs out you'll need to rely on those skills.

- Have an escape plan. If your neighborhood becomes dangerous or chaotic, have a plan of where you'll go and how you'll get there. A mountain bike may be your best friend during a global blackout.

- Stock up on light sources and batteries (in the hopes that batteries still work). Light sources include flashlights and headlamps as well as candles, glow sticks, and lanterns.

- Don't expect a lot of help. Police and fire departments will be overwhelmed. Hospitals may fill up quickly. You may have to rely on yourself and your loved ones until the crisis passes.

- Get good at building fires. With no electric light and no electric heat, a roaring fire can be your best friend.

- Be wary of strangers. Desperate times can cause even good people to make poor choices. And it makes the bad ones even worse! Trust the people you love, but watch your back with others.

- Keep a passion for reading. No more movies, TV, or video games for you. A good book may be the best entertainment you'll get for a while.

# GLOSSARY

**APPRENTICE** (uh-PREN-tiss)—a person who works for and learns from a skilled professional

**CULT** (KULT)—a particular form of religious devotion that involves deluded thinking and is often centered around a very charming and controlling leader

**ELECTROMAGNETIC PULSE** (i-lek-troh-mag-NET-ik PULS)—a sudden, powerful burst of energy capable of wiping out all electronics in an area; also called an EMP

**ISOLATION** (eye-suh-LAY-shuhn)—the condition of being alone or apart from others

**LOOT** (LOOT)—to steal from stores or houses during wartime or after a disaster

**MILITIA** (muh-LISH-uh)—a group of citizens who are trained to fight, but who only serve in an emergency

**SOLAR FLARE** (SOH-lur FLAYR)—an eruption of high-energy, magnetized gas from the Sun's surface

**SUPERCOLLIDER** (SOOP-ur-coll-eye-duhr)—a long tunnel lined with ultra-powerful magnets that accelerate tiny particles to amazing speeds; scientists cause these fast particles to collide, allowing them to be studied

**SUPERNOVA** (SOOP-ur-no-vuh)—the explosion of a massive star

**TOURNIQUET** (TUR-nuh-ket)—a tight wrapping designed to prevent a major loss of blood from a wound

# READ MORE

**Challoner, Jack.** *Energy.* New York: DK, 2012.

**Herweck, Don.** *Energy.* Mankato, Minn.: Compass Point Books, 2009.

**Miller, Ron.** *Is the End of the World Near? From Crackpot Predictions to Scientific Scenarios.* Minneapolis: Twenty-First Century Books, 2012.

**Spilsbury, Louise, and Richard Spilsbury.** *Electricity.* Chicago: Heinemann Library, 2014.

**Taylor-Butler, Christine.** *The Sun.* New York: Children's Press, 2014.

# INTERNET SITES

Use FactHound to find Internet sites related to this book. All of the sites on FactHound have been researched by our staff.

Here's all you do:
Visit *www.facthound.com*
Type in this code: 9781491458501

# AUTHOR

Matt Doeden is the author of more than 200 children's fiction and non-fiction books. A lifelong fan of science fiction and "what if" stories, he lives in Minnesota with his wife and two children.

# ILLUSTRATOR

James Nathan attended Worcester College of Art and Design in England and received a degree in Illustration at Cardiff School of Art and Design. His artwork is mostly fantasy and science fiction based, inspired by Pixar illustrations as well as the artist Dan LuVisi. James lives in Bristol, England, with his girlfriend and cat. In his spare time he enjoys making music, as well as music videos.